Jacob E. Green

JIMMY PAGE

MASTER OF THE GUITAR; FROM SESSION MUSICIAN TO ROCK
LEGEND

Jacob E. Green

Jacob E. Green

ı

Jacob E. Green

CU01503444

TABLE OF CONTENTS

INTRODUCTION

Have you ever heard a guitar played so amazingly that it almost feels like magic? Well, that's what it's like when Jimmy Page picks up a guitar! Jimmy Page is one of the best guitarists in the world, known for creating some of the most famous rock songs ever. He became a celebrity as the leader of the band Led Zeppelin, but his love for music started when he was just a kid like you.

Jimmy wasn't always a hero. He had to practice a lot and work hard to become the guitar hero we know today. Along the way, he found new ways to make the guitar sound exciting and powerful, inspiring other musicians and fans everywhere. Whether he was playing fast solos, soft melodies, or experimenting with new sounds, Jimmy always added something special to his music.

In this book, you'll learn all about Jimmy Page's trip from a young boy learning to play to becoming one of the most famous rock stars in history. Are you ready to rock? Let's dive into the world of Jimmy Page, the guitar star!

CHAPTER 1: YOUNG JIMMY

Jimmy Page was born on January 9, 1944, in a small town called Heston in England. As a boy, Jimmy was curious about the world around him. He loved drawing, reading, and discovering nature. But it wasn't until he was about 12 years old that something magical happened—he found the guitar.

One day, a family friend left an old guitar at Jimmy's house. Jimmy didn't know how to play it at first, but that didn't stop him! He was fascinated by the instrument. He began teaching himself how to play, playing the strings, and figuring out different sounds. Even though it was tough in the beginning, Jimmy didn't give up. The more he practiced, he became better.

At the time, rock 'n' roll music was becoming very famous. Jimmy loved listening to great guitarists like Elvis Presley's guitarist, Scotty Moore, and Chuck Berry. Their fast, energetic music motivated him to practice even more. Jimmy would spend hours with his guitar, trying to play along with his favorite songs.

But Jimmy didn't just listen to one kind of music. He loved blues, which is a style of music that's slow and full of feeling. He also liked folk music, which used soft, simple melodies. All these different types of music helped shape Jimmy's unique style.

As he got better, Jimmy's love for the guitar grew stronger. He began to dream of one day becoming a skilled musician. He played for his friends at school and started thinking about joining a band. Little did Jimmy know that this small dream would soon grow into something much, much bigger.

Jimmy's early life was all about curiosity, hard work, and a love for music. His passion for the guitar set him on a path that would change his life forever. Just a few years after he began playing, Jimmy Page would become one of the most famous guitar players in the world!

CHAPTER 2: LEARNING THE GUITAR

When Jimmy Page first picked up a guitar, he wasn't suddenly amazing. Like anyone learning something new, he had to start from the beginning. But what made Jimmy special was his determination and love for music. He didn't mind practicing for hours because he loved the way the guitar sounded, and he wanted to get better every day.

At first, Jimmy taught himself how to play. He didn't have a lot of lessons, so he would listen closely to the radio and music to figure out songs by ear. This means that instead of reading musical notes, Jimmy used his sharp ears to hear the sounds and then tried to play them on his guitar. It wasn't easy, but Jimmy was patient, and he kept playing until he could play along with his favorite songs.

One of the first songs he learned to play was "Baby Let's Play House" by Elvis Presley. It wasn't long before Jimmy was learning other rock 'n' roll tunes. But Jimmy wasn't just copying other guitar players—he was playing and finding his style, mixing different types of music like rock, blues, and folk.

By the time he was a teenager, Jimmy had become so good at guitar that people noticed his ability. He started playing with other young musicians and even performed at neighborhood events and parties. Jimmy loved the feeling of playing live in front of people.

Soon, Jimmy was introduced to some professional guitarists, and he took a few lessons to improve his skills even more. But even without any official lessons, Jimmy's ability to learn quickly and play with passion made him stand out. He tried different techniques and even experimented with using different objects, like a violin bow, to play his guitar in new and interesting ways!

Learning the guitar wasn't always easy, but Jimmy's love for the instrument pushed him to keep going. His fingers got faster, his strumming improved, and his creativity grew with every note. Before long, Jimmy Page wasn't just a kid playing for fun—he was on his way to becoming a guitar master. This was just t the beginning of an amazing journey in music!

CHAPTER 3: THE YARDBIRDS

By the time Jimmy Page became a teenager, he was known as a bright young guitarist. He played in small bands with friends and did studio work, where he helped record songs for other artists. But Jimmy's big break came when he joined a famous band called The Yardbirds.

The Yardbirds were already famous for their bluesy rock sound and had two great guitarists before Jimmy joined—Eric Clapton and Jeff Beck. When Jeff Beck chose to leave the band, The Yardbirds asked Jimmy Page to join them. Jimmy, excited to play with such a popular group, said yes! This was a big moment in his career because now he was playing with one of the best-known bands in England.

Jimmy started with The Yardbirds in 1966, and he fit right in. The band was known for playing a mix of blues and rock music, which was perfect for Jimmy's style. The Yardbirds also liked to experiment with new sounds and ideas, and Jimmy was great at that. He used all kinds of cool techniques, like playing the guitar with a violin bow, to make the music sound different and exciting.

One of Jimmy's first big shows with The Yardbirds was a European tour. This meant traveling around to different countries to play concerts for excited fans. Jimmy loved performing on stage, and he quickly became known for his incredible guitar solos, where he played fast, complicated melodies in the middle of songs. The crowd loved him!

With Jimmy in the band, The Yardbirds made songs like "Happenings Ten Years Ago" and "Little Games." Jimmy brought his taste to the music, mixing hard rock with psychedelic sounds. Although The Yardbirds were doing well, the band started having problems, and the other members chose to leave. This could have been the end of Jimmy's music career, but instead, it was a new starting.

When The Yardbirds broke up in 1968, Jimmy didn't give up on his dreams. He chose to start his band—one that would take everything he learned from The Yardbirds and go even further. That band would soon become Led Zeppelin, one of the best rock bands of all time!

The Yardbirds was Jimmy Page's first big band, and it helped him grow as a guitarist. He learned how to act in front of huge crowds, how to experiment with music, and how to be a leader. Even though his time with The Yardbirds wasn't very long, it was the first step toward Jimmy becoming a rock hero.

CHAPTER 4: THE BIRTH OF LED ZEPPELIN

When The Yardbirds broke up in 1968, Jimmy Page had a choice to make. He could either go back to playing for other people, or he could start something completely new. Jimmy wasn't ready to give up on his dream of being in a great band, so he chose to start his group. Little did he know, he was about to start one of the most famous rock bands in history—Led Zeppelin.

Jimmy's goal for the new band was clear. He wanted to make music that was loud, powerful, and different from anything else people were hearing at the time. He didn't want to be just another rock band—he wanted Led Zeppelin to mix rock, blues, and even folk music to make something completely special.

First, Jimmy needed to find the right performers to join him. He started by asking John Paul Jones, a skilled bass player and keyboardist, to join the band. John Paul Jones had worked with Jimmy before in recording studios, so Jimmy knew he was the right fit.

Next, Jimmy needed a singer. He was exposed to a young, unknown vocalist named Robert Plant, who had a voice that was both powerful and emotional. Robert Plant also shared Jimmy's love for blues and folk music, so they quickly became a great team.

Finally, the band needed a drummer—someone who could match the intensity and energy of the music Jimmy wanted to make. Robert Plant suggested his friend John Bonham, a drummer with amazing skills and a hard-hitting style. With John Bonham on drums, the band was complete.

At first, they called themselves the "New Yardbirds," since Jimmy was the last member of The Yardbirds. But soon after, they chose to change their name to Led Zeppelin, which was inspired by a joke that their music would go down "like a lead balloon" (meaning it would fail). Instead of letting that idea stop them, they made it into something powerful and memorable—Led Zeppelin was born!

In 1968, the newly formed band went into the studio to make their first album. Jimmy Page, who also acted as the band's manager, worked hard to make sure the music was exactly what he envisioned. They recorded songs like "Good Times Bad Times" and "Dazed and Confused," which showed off their hard rock sound and their ability to play with different styles.

When their first album, titled Led Zeppelin, was launched in 1969, it was a huge hit! People had never heard anything quite like it before. Jimmy's powerful guitar riffs, Robert Plant's soaring vocals, John Paul Jones' solid bass, and John Bonham's thunderous drumming produced a sound that was loud, bold, and exciting.

Led Zeppelin quickly became known for their energetic live shows. They toured across the world, playing to huge crowds who loved their music. Jimmy Page would often perform long guitar solos, while the rest of the band jammed together on stage, creating memorable moments for their fans.

From that moment on, Led Zeppelin was unbeatable. Over the next few years, they would release more albums filled with classic songs like "Whole Lotta Love," "Stairway to Heaven," and "Immigrant Song." Each album showed off their incredible skill and creativity, solidifying their place as one of the greatest rock bands ever.

The birth of Led Zeppelin wasn't just the beginning of a new band—it was the start of a musical change. Jimmy Page's dream of making something unique had come true, and Led Zeppelin became one of the is the most influential rock band in history.

CHAPTER 5: ROCKING THE WORLD

After the birth of Led Zeppelin, the band quickly began to rise to the top of the rock music world. Their first album was a huge hit, but this was just the beginning of their journey. In the late 1960s and early 1970s, Led Zeppelin went from being a new band to becoming one of the biggest and most important rock groups ever.

With their mix of hard rock, blues, and even folk music, Led Zeppelin's sound was unique and exciting. Fans loved the energy in their songs, the way Robert Plant's voice soared over Jimmy Page's powerful guitar riffs, and the thunderous rhythm given by John Paul Jones on bass and John Bonham on drums. Together, they made music that no one had ever heard before.

Their second record, Led Zeppelin II, was released in 1969 and it was an even bigger hit. The record featured the famous song "Whole Lotta Love," which became one of their signature tracks. It was loud, wild, and full of energy, showing off everything the band could do. Fans around the world were hooked!

But Led Zeppelin wasn't just great in the studio—they were also known for their amazing live performances. The band quickly became famous for putting on huge, energetic shows where they would play their songs for hours, often improvising and jamming together on stage. Jimmy Page would play long, amazing guitar solos, sometimes using a violin bow to make strange and exciting sounds, while Robert Plant would belt out words with his powerful voice. John Bonham's drumming was loud and fast, keeping the beat while John Paul Jones added deep bass sounds.

Their concerts were so famous that they sold out massive arenas all over the world, from the United States to Japan to Europe. Crowds would fill stadiums just to see Led Zeppelin play. Their tours were so popular that they often set new records for ticket sales. The band was now officially rocking the world!

In 1971, Led Zeppelin released what would become their most famous album: Led Zeppelin IV. This album included their biggest hit, "Stairway to Heaven." The song starts soft and mysterious, with an acoustic guitar, and builds up into a strong, hard-rock anthem. "Stairway to Heaven" became one of the most famous rock songs of all time, and people still listen to it today. The record also featured other classics like "Black Dog" and "Rock and Roll," which showed the band's ability to mix different styles into something new.

During the early 1970s, Led Zeppelin continued to release more records, each one filled with exciting and creative songs. Albums like Houses of the Holy and Physical Graffiti were packed with hits, and the band kept playing with different sounds. Sometimes they added folk influences, like in the song "The Battle of Evermore," or brought in exotic instruments to make new music.

But it wasn't just the music that made Led Zeppelin so famous—it was also their larger-than-life characters. The band members became rock stars in every way. They toured the world in private jets, stayed in fancy hotels, and became known for their wild and adventurous lifestyles. Jimmy Page, with his mysterious style and incredible guitar skills, became a rock star, while Robert Plant's stage presence and charisma made him one of the most famous frontmen in rock history.

As Led Zeppelin's popularity grew, so did their status as one of the best live bands in the world. Their shows were legendary, often lasting hours with intense energy from start to finish. Fans couldn't get enough, and the band played to sold-out crowds wherever they went.

By the mid-1970s, Led Zeppelin was on top of the world. They achieved everything they set out to do and even more. They weren't just a rock band anymore—they were a global phenomenon, with millions of fans all over the world. Their music was inspiring other artists, and their albums were selling millions of copies.

But even with all their success, Led Zeppelin never stopped pushing the limits of what rock music could be. They kept experimenting with new sounds, exploring different styles, and making music that was always exciting and fresh. Their rise to the top wasn't just about fame—it was about their love for music and their desire to keep rocking the world!

Jacob E. Green

CHAPTER 6: FAMOUS SONGS AND GUITAR SOLOS

Jimmy Page is known as one of the best guitar players in rock history, and a big part of that comes from his incredible songs and unforgettable guitar solos. As the head of Led Zeppelin, Jimmy wrote some of the most famous rock songs ever, and his guitar playing was a huge reason why people loved the band so much. Let's take a look at some of his most famous songs and the epic guitar riffs that made them legendary.

1. Whole Lotta Love
One of Led Zeppelin's most famous songs, "Whole Lotta Love," is filled with powerful guitar riffs. A riff is a short, repeated piece of music that's catchy and often the most recognizable part of the song. Jimmy Page came up with the opening riff for "Whole Lotta Love," and it became one of the most famous riffs in rock music history.

But what really stands out in this song is the wild and experimental guitar solo in the middle. Jimmy used all sorts of tricks to make strange, echoing sounds, giving the song a psychedelic feel. He even used a special guitar instrument called a theremin, which lets you control the sound without touching anything, making the solo sound otherworldly!

Jacob E. Green

2. Stairway to Heaven If there's one song that defines Led Zeppelin, it's "Stairway to Heaven." This song has it all—soft, beautiful parts, hard rock sections, and of course, one of the most famous guitar riffs ever. The song starts with an acoustic guitar, played softly and sweetly, but as it builds, the electric guitar takes over.

At the end of the song, Jimmy launches into a soaring, emotional guitar solo that is considered one of the best of all time. It's fast, powerful, and perfectly fits the rising intensity of the music. Fans loved this solo so much that "Stairway to Heaven" became one of the most requested songs at shows and on the radio.

3. Black Dog "Black Dog" is another Led Zeppelin hit that shows Jimmy Page's incredible guitar skills. The song is known for its complex rhythm, and Jimmy's riff in this song is heavy, bluesy, and difficult to play. It twists and turns, making it hard for even experienced players to follow.

Though "Black Dog" doesn't have a long break, the intricate guitar work throughout the song is what makes it stand out. Jimmy's fast fingerwork and unique playing style make this song a fan favorite.

4. Dazed and Confused "Dazed and Confused" is one of Led Zeppelin's early hits and features one of Jimmy Page's most experimental guitar performances. In live performances, Jimmy would often play this song with a violin bow instead of a guitar pick, making eerie, haunting sounds that no one had ever heard from a guitar before.

The solo in "Dazed and Confused" is wild and free, full of improvisation, which means Jimmy would often make up parts of it on the spot during live performances. The way he used different techniques to make strange and exciting sounds made this one of the most interesting and unforgettable solos in rock history.

5. Heartbreaker

If you want to hear Jimmy Page show off his guitar skills, listen to "Heartbreaker." This song has a famous guitar jam that is played completely without any backing music—just Jimmy and his guitar. This solo is fast, technical, and full of energy, showing just how skilled Jimmy Page was.

The solo in "Heartbreaker" has inspired countless guitarists to try and match Jimmy's speed and accuracy. It's one of the best examples of how Jimmy could blend blues and rock into something new and exciting.

6. Immigrant Song

With its driving beat and powerful singing from Robert Plant, "Immigrant Song" is one of Led Zeppelin's most energetic songs. Jimmy Page's guitar playing in this song is sharp and aggressive, matching the fast pace of the music. While the song doesn't feature a long solo, the opening riff is one of Jimmy's most famous works.

This song became so famous that it has been used in movies, commercials, and TV shows, continuing to remind people of Jimmy Page's brilliant guitar work.

7. Since I've Been Loving You

Jacob E. Green

This bluesy song, "Since I've Been Loving You," is a great example of Jimmy Page's emotional guitar playing. The guitar in this song isn't just loud and fast—it's full of feeling. The slow, passionate solo in the middle of the song shows off Jimmy's ability to make his guitar sing with feeling.

Jimmy's blues roots are strong in this song, and the solo is filled with bending notes and long, soulful phrases. This song shows that great guitar playing isn't just about being fast—it's about making every note count.

Jimmy's Legacy as a Guitar Hero
Jimmy Page's famous songs and guitar solos have influenced generations of musicians. His ability to mix hard rock with blues, folk, and even experimental sounds made him a true guitar hero. Whether he was playing lightning-fast solos or slow, emotional melodies, Jimmy Page always brought something new and exciting to Led Zeppelin's music.

His creativity, passion, and skill made songs like "Whole Lotta Love," "Stairway to Heaven," and "Heartbreaker" timeless favorites that people still love to listen to today. Jimmy Page's guitar playing will always be known as some of the greatest in rock history!

CHAPTER 7: JIMMY'S COOL GUITARS

When you think of Jimmy Page, the amazing guitarist from Led Zeppelin, you can't help but think about his incredible guitars! Just like a painter needs the right brushes to create beautiful artwork, Jimmy needs special guitars to make his awesome music. Let's take a closer look at some of the cool guitars that helped Jimmy become a rock legend!

1. The Gibson Les Paul

One of Jimmy's favorite guitars is the Gibson Les Paul. This guitar is famous for its thick, rich sound, and it has been used by many rock stars. Jimmy loved the way it looked and sounded, especially for his powerful riffs and leads. The Les Paul is heavy and solid, which helps create that deep, punchy sound that fans love. You can hear this guitar on songs like "Whole Lotta Love" and "Heartbreaker."

2. The Fender Telecaster

Before he started using the Les Paul, Jimmy often played a Fender Telecaster. This guitar has a bright, sharp sound that's great for rock music. It's lighter and easier to handle, which made it great for Jimmy when he was playing fast solos. He used the Telecaster in songs like "Good Times Bad Times" and even during his time with The Yardbirds.

Jacob E. Green

3. The Gibson EDS-1275
One of the coolest guitars Jimmy played is the Gibson EDS-1275. This guitar is unique because it has two necks! That means it has two sets of strings and frets, so Jimmy could switch between different sounds without having to grab another guitar. This guitar helped him create incredible moments during live performances, especially in songs like "Stairway to Heaven."

4. The Martin Acoustic Guitar
Jimmy didn't just love electric guitars; he also enjoyed playing acoustic guitars, especially a Martin acoustic guitar. Acoustic guitars have a warm, natural sound, perfect for softer songs. You can hear Jimmy playing his Martin in songs like "Babe I'm Gonna Leave You," where he strums slowly to create a beautiful melody. This shows how versatile Jimmy is as a musician!

5. The Danelectro
Another unique guitar that Jimmy used is the Danelectro. This guitar has a quirky, retro look and a bright sound that stands out. Jimmy liked to use it for its special tones, especially in live shows. The Danelectro helped him make interesting sounds that you wouldn't find with other guitars.

6. The Violin Bow

While not a guitar, one of the coolest things Jimmy Page did was use a violin bow on his electric guitar! By rubbing the bow against the strings, he could create eerie, haunting sounds that amazed fans. This technique can be heard in the song "Dazed and Confused," where Jimmy's creativity shines through, showing how he turned a simple guitar into something magical.

Jimmy's Love for Guitars

Jimmy Page's guitars were more than just instruments—they were his tools for expressing emotions and creating unforgettable music. He has said that each guitar has its personality, just like people. Some guitars are bright and cheerful, while others are deep and moody. Jimmy took great care of his guitars, knowing they were key to his sound.

As he traveled the world with Led Zeppelin, Jimmy brought his favorite guitars along for the ride. He would use them to create powerful music that connected with fans everywhere. His love for guitars inspired many young musicians to pick up an instrument and start playing.

The Legacy of Jimmy's Guitars

Today, Jimmy Page is known not only for his incredible skills as a guitarist but also for his amazing collection of guitars. His instruments are considered legendary, and many guitarists dream of playing a guitar just like his.

Through his unique sound and style, Jimmy Page helped shape rock music and left a mark that will never be forgotten. So next time you hear a Led Zeppelin song, remember the cool guitars that helped make that awesome sound. Jimmy Page and his guitars are truly a match made in rock 'n' roll heaven!

CHAPTER 8: ON THE ROAD

When Led Zeppelin became popular, they didn't just sit around at home; they hit the road and went on epic tours around the world! These trips were full of excitement, adventure, and unforgettable concerts. Let's dive into the incredible journeys that Led Zeppelin took and the amazing experiences they had while playing for fans everywhere.

1. The First Tour

After the release of their first record, Led Zeppelin, in 1969, the band set out on their first big tour. They played in the United States, performing in places like New York, Chicago, and San Francisco. Crowds filled the stadiums, eager to hear the new music from this rising rock band. Their shows were filled with energy, and fans went wild as Jimmy Page's guitar riffs rang out and Robert Plant sang with passion.

During this first tour, Led Zeppelin quickly learned how to connect with their fans. They played longer sets, jamming together and making each show special. This made every show a special experience for fans, who left feeling thrilled and eager for more.

2. The Legendary Shows

As Led Zeppelin gained more fame, their concerts became legendary. They played in some of the biggest arenas in the world, including Madison Square Garden in New York City and the Royal Albert Hall in London. Fans would often line up for hours just to get tickets to see them live!

One of their most famous shows took place at Royal Albert Hall in 1970. The show was full of energy, and it included incredible solos from Jimmy Page and powerful vocals from Robert Plant. This show was recorded and is still celebrated today as one of the best live performances in rock history.

3. The World Tours

Led Zeppelin didn't just stick to the United States. They traveled all over the world, playing in places like Europe, Japan, Australia, and even the Middle East! Each tour was an adventure, as they explored different cultures and met fans from all walks of life.

In 1972, they went on a massive tour called the "United States Tour." This tour was important because it solidified their position as one of the biggest rock bands in the world. They played to huge crowds, sometimes playing two shows in one day! During the shows, Jimmy would often improvise, playing extended guitar solos that left crowds cheering for more.

4. The Private Jet

As Led Zeppelin's fame grew, so did their lifestyle. They often went in a private jet called the "Starship," which was decorated like a luxury lounge. This allowed the band to move comfortably and quickly from city to city. They would enjoy meals, relax, and have fun while flying to their next show.

Jacob E. Green

However, with the luxury came wild experiences. The band members were known for their fun-loving and sometimes mischievous behavior on the road. They had a reputation for having wild parties and enjoying their success to the fullest. These adventures often made for famous stories that fans would talk about for years!

5. The Fans

One of the best parts of traveling for Led Zeppelin was meeting their fans. The band loved the energy of the crowd and the excitement that filled the stadiums. Fans would scream, cheer, and sing along to every song, creating an electric atmosphere at each show.

Led Zeppelin also built a loyal fanbase that went from city to city just to see them play. These fans were dedicated, often camping out for days to gain the best spots in the front row. The bond between the band and their fans got stronger with each show, creating unforgettable memories for everyone involved.

6. The End of an Era

After years of touring and making music together, Led Zeppelin's journey on the road began to change. Sadly, in 1980, sadness struck when drummer John Bonham passed away. The band chose to disband, knowing they could never perform without him. Their last tour in 1979 was a bittersweet farewell to an incredible age in rock music.

Even though Led Zeppelin's touring days came to an end, the memories of their epic concerts and trips around the world live on. They changed the way rock bands performed and left a legacy that continues to inspire musicians today.

The Impact of Their Tours

Led Zeppelin's epic trips were not just about playing music; they were about sharing experiences, making memories, and connecting with fans. Each show was a celebration of rock music, and every adventure on the road added to their story as one of the greatest bands in history.

Their tours left a lasting influence on the music world and set the stage for future bands to follow in their footsteps. Led Zeppelin showed everyone that rock 'n' roll was not just a genre; it was a way of life—full of excitement, adventure, and amazing moments!

CHAPTER 9: CHALLENGES AND CHANGES

After years of success and unforgettable music, Led Zeppelin faced some tough challenges that finally led to the end of the band. While their trip had been filled with excitement, fame, and legendary performances, some difficulties tested the members' strength and friendship. Let's take a closer look at these difficulties and the changes that marked the end of Led Zeppelin.

1. The Pressure of Fame

As Led Zeppelin grew in fame, the pressure to keep up with their success became overwhelming. They had made some of the most famous rock songs in history, and fans everywhere expected them to continue delivering more incredible music. This pressure made it hard for the band members to relax and enjoy their success.

In the early 1970s, they were traveling non-stop, playing in different countries almost every night. While they loved playing for their fans, the grueling schedule started to take a toll on their health and relationships. Being in the spotlight can be exciting, but it also comes with its difficulties.

2. Personal Struggles

Each member of Led Zeppelin faced personal problems during the height of their fame. Robert Plant, the lead singer, dealt with the pressure of being the face of the band and the weight of expectations from fans and reviewers. Jimmy Page, the brilliant guitarist, struggled with the responsibilities of being in a top band and balancing his personal life.

John Paul Jones, the bassist and keyboardist, often felt overshadowed by the more flamboyant personalities in the band, which made it difficult for him to show his creativity. Meanwhile, John Bonham, the drummer, was battling personal problems and substance abuse. These struggles caused tension within the band and affected their ability to work together as a cohesive unit.

3. Tragedy Strikes

The most devastating challenge came in September 1980 when John Bonham sadly passed away. His death was a huge shock to everyone, especially to his friends. John was not only a skilled drummer but also a close friend to Jimmy, Robert, and John Paul. Losing him felt like losing a part of themselves, and it changed everything for the band.

Bonham's death left a giant hole in Led Zeppelin, and the band members were crushed. They understood that they could never continue without him, as he was a crucial part of their sound and spirit. The laughter and camaraderie they once shared started to fade, replaced by grief and doubt.

4. The Decision to Disband

In the wake of Bonham's passing, the surviving members of Led Zeppelin faced a difficult choice. After much discussion, they agreed to disband in December 1980. They felt that Led Zeppelin could never be the same without their beloved drummer. It was a tough choice for all of them, as they had spent so many years creating music and playing together.

While they knew it was the right choice, it was also a heartbreaking one. They had built an amazing legacy and made music that inspired millions, but the bond they shared was shattered by tragedy.

5. Life After Led Zeppelin

After the band broke up, each member went on to follow their projects and interests. Robert Plant made solo albums and explored different musical styles. Jimmy Page worked with other artists, including forming a new band called The Firm. John Paul Jones worked on different musical projects, including producing and writing music for other artists.

Although they found success in their solo lives, the members of Led Zeppelin always held a special place in their hearts for the music they created together. They sometimes reflected on their time as a band and the memories they shared, but the loss of Bonham made it tough to think about reuniting.

6. The Legacy Lives On

Even though Led Zeppelin officially stopped in 1980, their music never faded away. Songs like "Stairway to Heaven," "Whole Lotta Love," and "Black Dog" continue to inspire new generations of singers and fans. Led Zeppelin remains one of the most famous rock bands in history, and their albums are still loved and listened to all around the world.

Over the years, the surviving members have rarely reunited for special performances, reminding fans of the magic they created together. The 2007 reunion concert in London was a highlight, showcasing the band's incredible ability one last time.

Conclusion

The end of Led Zeppelin was a difficult chapter in the story of rock music, marked by challenges, changes, and sadness. Despite the tough times, the band's legacy goes on through their timeless music. Led Zeppelin showed the world what real rock and roll could be—full of passion, creativity, and unforgettable moments.

Their journey tells us that while challenges may come our way, the friendships we build and the music we create can last forever, leaving a mark on the hearts of fans for generations to come.

Jacob E. Green

CHAPTER 10: JIMMY'S LIFE AFTER LED ZEPPELIN

After the end of Led Zeppelin in 1980, Jimmy Page faced a new stage in his life.
Although he had found tremendous success with the band, he now had the
opportunity to explore new musical paths and personal interests. Let's take a look
at what Jimmy did after Led Zeppelin and how he continued to make his mark in
the world of music.

1. A Period of Reflection
In the years immediately following Led Zeppelin's breakup, Jimmy took time to
reflect on his work and personal life. The loss of his dear friend and bandmate,
John Bonham, weighed deeply on him. He needed time to process the band's end
and what it meant for his future. During this time, he also focused on his family
and personal interests, rediscovering his love for music in a more relaxed way.

2. Collaborating with Other Artists
As Jimmy began to feel ready to return to music, he started collaborating with
different artists. In 1982, he worked with ex Free and Bad Company singer Paul
Rodgers to form a band called The Firm. The Firm produced two albums, The Firm
and Mean Business, which featured a blend of hard rock and pop elements. Songs
like "Radioactive" and "Satisfaction Guaranteed" highlighted Jimmy's iconic guitar
work and introduced him to a new generation of fans.

3. Solo Projects

In addition to his work with The Firm, Jimmy Page also took on solo projects. In 1987, he released a solo album named Outrider, which included tracks like "Wasting My Time" and "Stairway to Heaven (Live)." This album showed his unique guitar style and allowed him to experiment with different sounds. He also toured to promote the record, delighting fans with his incredible live performances.

4. Collaborating with Robert Plant

In the mid-1990s, Jimmy reunited with Robert Plant for a number of successful projects. The duo released the record *No Quarter: Jimmy Page and Robert Plant Unledded* in 1994, which featured a mix of Led Zeppelin classics and new material. The album was well-received, and they went on a tour that brought together old and new fans alike. The collaboration showed that the magic between them was still alive, and their chemistry on stage was undeniable.

5. Film Soundtracks and Other Projects

Jimmy Page also contributed his guitar skills to different film soundtracks. In 1998, he worked on the soundtrack for the film The Crow: City of Angels, showing his ability to blend rock with different musical styles. He was involved in different musical projects, including producing and working with emerging artists, helping to shape the next generation of musicians.

6. The 2007 Reunion Concert

One of the most important moments in Jimmy's life after Led Zeppelin came in 2007 when the surviving members reunited for a special concert at the O2 Arena in London. This performance was a salute to their late drummer, John Bonham, and marked their first live performance together in nearly three decades. Fans were

Jacob E. Green

thrilled to see the legendary band come together again, and the concert was met
with widespread acclaim, proving that their music still resonated strongly with
audiences.

7. A Legacy of Influence

Throughout the years, Jimmy Page has been a highly influential figure in rock
music. He has inspired countless artists with his innovative guitar techniques and
songwriting skills. Many young musicians look up to him as a role model, and his
work continues to shape the sound of rock music today.

8. Continuing to Create

Even after all these years, Jimmy Page has continued to work on different musical
projects. He has released remastered versions of Led Zeppelin's classic albums and
participated in documentaries and interviews that explore the band's impact on
music. Jimmy's passion for music has never faded, and he still likes playing and
creating in different ways.

Conclusion

Jimmy Page's life after Led Zeppelin was filled with new chances and exciting
projects. He explored his creativity, worked with talented artists, and remained a
vital force in the world of rock music. Though Led Zeppelin may have stopped,
Jimmy's journey as a musician continued, and he has left an indelible mark on the
history of music.

His story shows that while one part may close, many new adventures await. Jimmy
Page's love for music, passion for guitar, and ability to connect with fans have
made him a true rock legend, and his impact will last for generations to come.

CHAPTER 11: JIMMY PAGE'S LEGACY

Jimmy Page is not just a legendary guitarist; he is a musical icon whose impact continues to resonate across generations. His contributions to rock music, innovative techniques, and unique style have left an everlasting mark on the business. Let's explore why Jimmy Page is still famous today and what makes his impact so remarkable.

1. The Sound of Led Zeppelin

At the heart of Jimmy Page's reputation is his role as the guitarist and producer of Led Zeppelin. The band is often regarded as one of the best rock bands of all time, and their music defined an entire era. Songs like "Stairway to Heaven," "Whole Lotta Love," and "Black Dog" showcase Jimmy's exceptional guitar work, blending powerful riffs, complex solos, and innovative sound effects. These tracks continue to be played on radio stations and at parties, making them timeless classics that bring new fans to his music every day.

2. Innovative Guitar Techniques

Jimmy Page is known for his groundbreaking guitar techniques that have inspired countless artists. He was one of the first musicians to use distortion and feedback creatively, pushing the boundaries of what the electric guitar could do. His use of alternate tunings, slide guitar, and the famous violin bow method added unique sounds to his music that had never been heard before.

Many guitarists today study Page's work to learn his skills and understand his approach to songwriting. He made sounds that were revolutionary for his time, influencing a wide range of genres, from hard rock to heavy metal.

3. A Master of Songwriting

In addition to his incredible guitar skills, Jimmy Page is also an excellent songwriter. He wrote many of Led Zeppelin's most famous songs, crafting melodies and arrangements that have captivated fans for decades. His ability to blend different musical styles, from blues to folk to rock, allowed Led Zeppelin to create a diverse catalog of music that appealed to many different audiences.

4. Iconic Collaborations

Throughout his career, Jimmy has collaborated with multiple artists and bands, further cementing his legacy in the music world. His partnerships with musicians like Robert Plant, David Coverdale, and Paul Rodgers introduced him to new audiences and showcased his versatility as an artist. These collaborations often brought out the best in both parties, leading to memorable songs and performances that fans still cherish.

5. A Role Model for Future Musicians

Jimmy Page has served as a role model for aspiring musicians around the world. His dedication to his craft, passion for music, and willingness to experiment have inspired countless artists to pursue their dreams. Many famous guitarists, including

Kirk Hammett of Metallica, Slash of Guns N' Roses, and Jack White, have cited Jimmy as one of their biggest influences.

Music schools and guitar teachers frequently use his songs as part of their lessons, introducing new generations to his genius and helping to keep his music alive.

6. Enduring Popularity and Cultural Impact

Jimmy Page's influence extends beyond music; he has become a cultural icon. Led Zeppelin's music has been featured in movies, commercials, and television shows, ensuring that new fans discover their songs every day. The band's mystique and Jimmy's larger-than-life persona have made them a part of rock 'n' roll history.

Additionally, Jimmy Page has appeared in various documentaries, interviews, and tribute concerts, sharing his experiences and insights with fans. His willingness to engage with the public and discuss his music has kept interest in him and Led Zeppelin alive.

7. Preservation of His Work

In recent years, the remastering and re-releasing of Led Zeppelin's albums have introduced their music to younger audiences. These releases highlight the band's innovative sound and Jimmy's incredible guitar work, ensuring that their legacy continues to thrive. Documentaries and books about Led Zeppelin also help to keep the band's history alive, celebrating their impact on music and culture.

Conclusion

Jimmy Page's legacy is built on his incredible talent, innovative spirit, and the timeless music he created with Led Zeppelin. His influence can still be heard in the music of countless artists today, and his status as one of the greatest guitarists of all time remains unchallenged.

As long as there are fans who love rock music, Jimmy Page's contributions will continue to be celebrated. His journey in the world of music serves as an inspiration for aspiring musicians everywhere, showing that with passion, creativity, and hard work, it's possible to leave a lasting impact on the world. Jimmy Page is not just a name in music history; he is a legend whose spirit will live on through his music for years to come.

CHAPTER 12: FUN FACTS ABOUT JIMMY PAGE

Jimmy Page is a rock legend known for his incredible guitar skills and the unforgettable music he created with Led Zeppelin. But there's more to him than just his time in the band! Here are some fun and surprising facts about Jimmy Page that you might not know.

1. He Started Young

Jimmy Page started playing guitar at a very young age. He picked up the instrument when he was just 12 years old! His early inspiration came from listening to rock and roll, blues, and folk music. He quickly fell in love with the guitar and dedicated himself to mastering it.

2. A Talented Musician Beyond Guitar

While he is best known as a guitarist, Jimmy Page is also a talented producer and arranger. He played a crucial role in producing Led Zeppelin's albums, helping to create their unique sound. Additionally, he can play other instruments, including the bass and keyboards, showcasing his versatility as a musician.

3. The Violin Bow Technique

One of Jimmy Page's most famous techniques is using a violin bow on his guitar. This unusual method creates a unique sound that adds texture to his music. He first used the bow during a live performance of "Dazed and Confused," and it became one of his signature moves. This creative approach influenced many other guitarists to experiment with different sounds.

4. A Love for the Occult

Jimmy Page has a fascination with the occult, particularly with the writings of Aleister Crowley, an influential figure in mysticism and magic. He even purchased Crowley's former home, Boleskine House, in Scotland. This interest in the mystical has sometimes been reflected in the lyrics and themes of Led Zeppelin's songs.

5. A Collector of Guitars

Jimmy Page is an avid guitar collector and owns an impressive collection of unique and rare guitars. One of his most famous guitars is a 1960 Gibson Les Paul Standard, which he used to record many of Led Zeppelin's greatest hits. His collection includes other instruments, such as Fender Telecasters and acoustic guitars, showcasing his love for various guitar styles.

6. A Brief Acting Role

Did you know that Jimmy Page made a brief appearance in a film? He had a cameo role in the 1976 movie The Song Remains the Same, which documents Led Zeppelin's concert at Madison Square Garden. The film features live performances and behind-the-scenes footage, giving fans a glimpse into the band's life on tour.

7. A Love for Folk Music

Before becoming a rock superstar, Jimmy Page had a deep appreciation for folk music. He was influenced by artists like Bob Dylan and The Beatles, which inspired some of Led Zeppelin's more melodic and acoustic tracks. Songs like

41

"Going to California" highlight his love for folk and showcase his skill as a songwriter.

8. Musical Influences

Jimmy Page's guitar style was influenced by a variety of musicians. He admired blues guitarists like B.B. King, Muddy Waters, and Howlin' Wolf. He was also inspired by rock and roll legends such as Chuck Berry and Elvis Presley. This blend of influences helped shape his unique sound and style.

9. Environmentalist

In addition to his musical talents, Jimmy Page is passionate about environmental issues. He has been involved in various charitable activities and has spoken out about the importance of protecting the environment. His love for nature shows his desire to make the world a better place.

10. The "Page" Turners

Jimmy Page has also dabbled in writing and has released books on music and guitar skills. He is known for sharing his experiences and knowledge, helping to inspire the next generation of musicians. His passion for teaching others shows that he cares deeply about the future of music.

Conclusion

Jimmy Page is more than just a rock legend; he is a fascinating individual with a rich history and diverse interests. From his innovative guitar techniques to his love for folk music and environmental advocacy, there's so much to discover about him. These fun facts remind us that behind the music, there's a unique and inspiring person who has made a lasting impact on the world of rock and roll.

Whether you're a long-time fan or just discovering his music, Jimmy Page's story continues to inspire and entertain fans all over the globe.

CHAPTER 13: WHAT WE CAN LEARN FROM JIMMY PAGE

Jimmy Page's journey from a young guitarist to a legendary rock star is filled with important lessons that can inspire us in many ways. Beyond his music, Jimmy's dedication, creativity, and determination show us how to chase our dreams and make a lasting effect. Let's explore some important things we can learn from the life of Jimmy Page.

1. Follow Your Passion

One of the biggest lessons we can learn from Jimmy Page is the value of following your passion. Jimmy found his love for music at a young age and dedicated himself to mastering the guitar. He didn't give up, even when things were tough. This passion drove him to become one of the best guitarists of all time.

Lesson: Whatever your interest may be—whether it's music, art, science, or sports—pursue it with enthusiasm. When you follow what you love, amazing things can happen.

2. Practice and Hard Work Pay Off

Jimmy Page didn't become a rock star overnight. He spent hours playing the guitar, learning different styles, and improving his skills. Even when he was already popular, Jimmy continued to work hard, always looking for ways to innovate and push the boundaries of music. His success is proof that practice and commitment are key to achieving your goals.

Lesson: Hard work and practice are important if you want to be great at something. Whether it's playing an instrument or learning a new skill, the more you practice, the better you'll become.

3. Be Creative and Think Outside the Box
Jimmy Page was known for his creativity and desire to try new things. He played with different guitar techniques, like playing with a violin bow, and incorporated various musical styles into Led Zeppelin's music. He wasn't afraid to take chances, and that's what made his music so special.

Lesson: Don't be afraid to think outside the box and try something new. Creativity comes from exploring different ideas and finding unique ways to present yourself. Sometimes, the best results come from taking risks and being open to new options.

4. Teamwork Makes a Difference
While Jimmy was an amazing guitarist, Led Zeppelin's success was a team effort. Each member of the band brought something special to the table, and they worked together to create their signature sound. Jimmy valued the input of his bandmates and knew that teamwork was important to their success.

Lesson: Whether you're working on a school project, playing in a band, or participating in a team sport, remember that teamwork is important. Everyone has strengths that can contribute to the overall success, and working together can lead to amazing results.

5. Overcoming Challenges

Throughout his career, Jimmy Page faced many challenges. The breakup of Led Zeppelin, the loss of his friend John Bonham, and personal struggles all tested him. But Jimmy didn't let these challenges stop him. He continued to create music, collaborate with other artists, and inspire fans around the world.

Lesson: Life is full of challenges, but it's important to keep moving forward. When things get tough, focus on your skills and keep working toward your goals. Challenges will make you stronger and help you grow.

6. Stay Humble

Despite his fame, Jimmy Page has always been known for his humble and down-to-earth personality. He never let his success go to his head, and he always showed respect for his fans and fellow musicians. His humility is part of what has made him so loved and admired.

Lesson: No matter how successful you become, it's important to stay humble. Treat others with kindness and respect, and remember where you came from. People will admire you not just for what you achieve, but for how you carry yourself.

7. Never Stop Learning

Even after decades of being in the music business, Jimmy Page never stopped learning. He always looked for new ways to improve his skills and try different musical styles. His curiosity and love for learning helped him stay creative and innovative throughout his work.

Lesson: Learning is a lifelong process. Whether it's in school or life, there is always something new to learn. Stay curious, keep asking questions, and never stop expanding your knowledge.

8. Embrace Your Uniqueness

Jimmy Page's guitar style was different from many other artists of his time. He didn't try to copy anyone else; instead, he embraced his unique sound and style. This made him stand out and become a true original in the world of music.

Lesson: Don't be afraid to be yourself and embrace what makes you unique. Everyone has their special talents and qualities, and by staying true to who you are, you can make your mark on the world.

Conclusion

Jimmy Page's journey is filled with lessons that go beyond music. His passion, creativity, and dedication teach us that with hard work and a love for what you do, anything is possible. By following his example, we can learn to overcome challenges, work as a team, and never stop striving to be the best version of ourselves.

Jimmy's life reminds us that no matter where you start, you have the power to build something amazing. Whether you're playing a guitar, writing a story, or chasing your dreams, always remember: that greatness comes from desire, hard work, and staying true to yourself.

CONCLUSION

Jimmy Page is more than just a guitar legend—he is a symbol of fire, creativity, and innovation. From his early days as a young boy fascinated by music to his time as the driving force behind Led Zeppelin, Jimmy's story is one of dedication and artistry. He changed the world of rock music with his iconic guitar riffs, groundbreaking techniques, and unforgettable songs that continue to inspire millions of fans.

Beyond his musical talent, Jimmy Page's story teaches us important life lessons about the importance of hard work, teamwork, and staying true to your unique self. He showed the world that success doesn't come without work and that pushing the boundaries of what's possible can lead to incredible achievements.

Jimmy's impact on music is still felt today, and his legacy will continue to inspire generations to come. Whether through his epic guitar solos, his creativity in songwriting, or his enduring love for music, Jimmy Page will always be known as one of the greatest rock stars in history. His journey tells us that with a pass ion and dedication, we can all leave our mark on the world.

Printed in Great Britain
by Amazon